Skulls & Roses

R. C. Seiner

BookLeaf
Publishing

India | USA | UK

Presentation by *BookLeaf Publishing*

Web: www.bookleafpub.com

E-mail: info@bookleafpub.com

ISBN: 978-93-5744-945-8

First edition 2022

DEDICATION

To Tyler

ACKNOWLEDGEMENT

Thank you Robin Carstensen, Chuck Etheridge, Marte Parham, and Meghan Brannon-Reese for helping me develop my creative writing skills. In addition, thank you to the team at BookLeaf Publishing for this opportunity.

The Black Birds Call

It came in a dream.
The haunting call of death's regime.
Mirrored twice, the black birds call,
waiting and seeking the other's fall.
The eyes of red
fills the eyes of green with dread.
If the two touch,
war ensures as such.
But if the mirror splits askew,
sight will reset anew.
Pride will question sight,
Fear will stop when right.
Those with power will see,
just how much is free.
If the mirror mends by force,
the core of one will take its course.
Destruction will befall one's life,
proof neither can live without strife.
Two hearts will separate,
but will merge at the set date.
Tears will fall in blood,
when the name is dragged through mud.

Sanity will fall unsealed,
when the truth is finally revealed.
The heart of the one,
will soothe the third son.
The evil dispersed
from the eternal curse.
Deception will be unseen
from the minds of green.
And eyes once filled with dread,
will be dyed forever in red.

Searching, Seeing

The Raven beats and bows against the shadows;
The inky blackness cut by small cracks of light.
Blood red eyes burn through the space,

Searching. Seeing. Saving.

Clutter and memories litter the floor;
Teardrops and sighs dance on the edge.
The Raven collapses to the blood-soaked wood.
Outside, the Crow watches.

Searching. Seeing. Sacrificing.

From Embers to Flames

The Fall was not quick.
It wasn't painless;
It wasn't easy.
The Stars weren't without sorrow.

The Sister,
The Darkness
Was the Curse;
Locked away from the Dawn.
The Brother,
The Light
Went away;
The Sons and Daughters
Were abandoned.

The Morning Star Rebelled,
And was cast down;
It held a grudge to Creation.
The Suns were at war
For the Throne;
The Garden was in Ruins

One Ember was the Savior.
It had a crack in the structure,
And did not conform.
It was shunned
Because it loved too much.

Each time it chose the Earth
And turned away from the Sky.
The Ember grew into a Blaze
In the Eyes of the One.

The Ember feared it would go out,
That it would not live for long.
The Sky sent rain,
The Earth changed,
Yet it survived from a Wish
And grew to a Flame.

The Fall was not quick,
It wasn't painless;
It wasn't easy.
But the Ember
Found a place to
Burn its warm light.
All because of a Wish.

Hotter than Hell, Thicker than Thieves

The air around me is thick and hot.
No, not the air.
The thick piece of cloth that absorbs
every drop of sweat, every salty tear,
every thought of fear and dread.
The only connection to the outside world
are two thick foggy circles of glass,
and tube that filters out the sweet and stinging
scents of the world around me.
I'm outside, yet in a small,
claustrophobic space.
I can barely make out the whizzing and
whistling
of missiles that zips around me,
or the continuous *dadadadada* of the bullets
flying
out of the guns of my already dead brothers.
Even the cold steel machine gun in front of me
Sounds far away.
Beside me, is another me.

The same head.
The same clothes.
The same smell of fear and desperation and
anger.
The same already-dead face.
We are outside,
but we are in hell.

Stillness

Weave

in,

weave

out.

A brush of breath exhales

One

and

a

two

and

a

three

and

a

four

and

a

one

and

a

two

and

a

three

and

a

four

Drip

Drip

Drip

A creak in the boards,

a frenzy of leaves

The faint crunch of the stones in the road

The bird above sings the song

The wind whips around

in time

One

and

a

two

and

a

three

and

a

four

and

a

one

and

a

two

and

a

three

and

a

four

Music plays in the Stillness

And the whole Town

Dances to the

Rhythm

One

and

a

two

and

a

three

and

a

four

and

a

one

and

a

two

and

a

three

and

a

four

Ghost White

Snow drifting in the air,
Slowly like the servants of Death.
Whispering a dangerous dare,
To the traveler to take her last breath.

The Chasm looms towards the sky,
Testing her strength of mind.
The scent of the challenge made her high,
Yet she knows the journey will not be kind.

A warning was told,
By the elder with a bitter frown,
Of a monster of old,
That stole people from the town.

"A terrible beast, with a body of ice,
Descended with the fire that fell from the sky.
Eyes of yellow that burned with vice,
and made one shudder with its hollow cry."

"To protect us from being the monster's feast,
We do not leave home after dark." Said she,
"Do not, young one, pursue the beast,
Or his next meal shall be thee."

The traveler scoffed at the tale,
"What a cowardly thing to say!
I shall catch the beast that makes you ail."
With a huff she left to the woman's dismay.

A smile all but fades at the sights she saw;
A mist of spirits, young and old,
warning of a beast that rose a mile tall.
The same tales the woman had foretold.

Through the cave she wanders,
Dark as night and black as pitch,
Through the stale air she ponders,
"Strange, this path gives me a twitch."

A light guides her out
Into a clearing of trees.
She thinks, "What a bizarre route,"
Before she drops to her knees.

As she falls to the ground,
A cold blanket descends.
A shadow lurks without a sound,
Leading her to a bitter end.

She wakes with a start,
Dizzy from the cold and her slumber.
She does not feel the thump of her heart;
She counts no number.

She stares at the skin of her hands
And flinches at the sight.
Blue as frost with icy bands,
Then screams with all her might.

Snow slowly drifts through the air,
Where she took her last breath.
She had fallen for nature's dangerous dare
and fell to the Master of Death.

Wind

Not one day passes that
the wind whips with razor-like sharpness.
White eyes close against the force
of a whip in hand that transforms into a
hard and thick wall of cellophane.
You've won when you could get through without
feeling the cotton suffocating your windpipe,
desiring relief.
Or rather something that will block out
the piercing wind as onlookers stare at the
pitiless victims from the inside of their haven.
Snow white eyes look on in sympathy.

Contradictions

The world is made of contradictions.

From birth, we are expected to follow our
dreams,
Yet we have to follow the path that authority sets
in place.
We are told in life to put in effort,
Yet we are scoffed at for being an overachiever.
We are told to be ourselves and to grow and
flourish that way,
Yet those who express themselves are shunned
and labeled as freaks.

In truth, we are not supposed to "be" our own
person.
We are expected to be a person who is
acceptable;
A fabricated image under the guise of "normal."
The world has gotten so involved with image
and reputations,
That the definition of normal has changed.

We are constantly told that we are not enough.
No matter how much effort we already apply.
If we want to succeed, we must follow the mold.

A test to see how "perfect" we can be.

17

On the Island

On the island
The birds sang their songs
and the trees bowed in the breeze.

On the island,
The gentle fountain flowed,
And the insects scurried across the concrete
stones.

On the island,
The wind scatters the leaves
And lifts the flowers with ease.

On the island,
The air becomes cooler
As the sun sets and dusk descends.

On the island,
The world is calm,
The sound of the waves echo as they ebb and
flow
Across the peaceful spot.

On the island,
Time is quiet.

Dream World

What is it that you see?
A flourishing green world?
Little flowers that dot the scene with colors?

No.
The ground is cracked,
The scene is brown.

Why are you crying?
Is it because you quit?
Are you so broken that you can't go on?

No
It is just the smoke in the air.

Are you going to swim?
Look at the water.
Is it a crystal blue that ebbs and flows against
the shore?
Is it clean that you can see the bottom?

No.
You are staring at mud and ash.

You think that the world is fine,

But you are living in a dream world.
Wake up
And plunge into the fire.

Let Go

When you let go of the past,
People become decorations
In the background.

When you let go of the present,
Your goals catch flame
and burn to ash.

When you let go of the future,
Time ceases and spirit stales
into the abyss of the mind.

To let go is to die.
To let go is to be free.
To let go is to be imprisoned.
To let go is to be alive.

When I hear the word "Scotland," I Think of the Color Green.

It's greener in Scotland. Much, much greener.

I want to return and live in the fantasy of being a stereotypical writer. Brooding by the river Esk, scribbling down whatever comes to mind. Being frozen in the stillness of the forest, zoning out and daydreaming.

Walking down the streets of Edinburgh, staring at an alleyway and imagining a murder. Glancing around a chapel and seeing a sacrifice. Looking at a structure, but seeing something else. Writing out scenes in my head until it was obvious on my face.

One day I will return.

Back to the rabbit hole.

Back to the past,

Back to the river.

If I hear the word Scotland, I'll think of the color
green.

The Angel's Mark

Until we know for sure,
we can't underestimate the other side.
The Angels know we have a mortal among us,
and they will stop at nothing to get her,
to free her.
We cannot succumb to their tricks;
We must protect her.
Her soul is the only thing that matters to us.
We can't let her fall into the Angels' hands.
Since she joined us in our house,
we have grown very fond of her.
Our number one rule is to serve and protect our
family.
And even though she is human,
She is family.
And we will defend her with our lives.

Death's Embrace

What say thee,
A river flows in tandem with an everlasting
glow.
From the soft sound of a bird's chirp,
And the whip of a hollow song.
Such is a glimmer of a rose's thorns,
And the sinful hum plays its verse.
Stop now and rest,
Let the lull of the night drift along,
And thus shall fall into such quiet slumber.
Ne'er to rise again.

Twitch

All these voices in my head won't stop.
Go Left? Go Right?
Which way is Up? Is that Down?
What is anarchy?
Democracy is evil?
Back and Forth
Left and Right
Endlessly. Dizzy.
My hands are moving on their own.
I have no will over their movements.
The voices are the law.
I must listen to the voices.
The voices control everything.
Over and Over!
A constant cycle.
Never to cease.

At the Beach

Waves crashed along the sand with a song
playing to its own rhythm.
The sharp aroma of the sea that hangs and creeps
weaves through the thick brush that hides the
lapis bay.
Hard-packed sand molds against each step;
a perfect indention to one who trudges along.
It's quiet, peaceful even.
The perfect place to think, create, or sit in
silence.

Salvation

What does it mean to just sit there and watch as those whom you care for struggle to find a way to survive? When the only consultation you can give is a few words and a simple hug?

You curse the heavens as you know you can't do anything to change. You can't take away their fear, even if you want to.

You worry that the world will end and you get caught in the middle. You're drained and just want to sleep.

Nations quake. Buildings fall. And you are the one to pick up the pieces.

But what happens if you can't even do that? You find yourself just floating in a black abyss while the world gets thrown into chaos. The memories haunt you. You just sit there in the dark as your world comes crashing down.

A cry for help. A cry for Salvation escapes your lips. And just when you start to lose heart, a ray of light cuts through the dark. You let the warm light embrace you, knowing you can finally be reunited with your loved ones.

But it never comes. Against anger, you drop. That light is not the sweet cradle of death. But Salvation comes regardless.

You can escape the situation, but you can't escape the feelings. Those will always chain you down, no matter how hard you fight. And so you are left with the feeling in the back of your head that you cannot change the course of your life, but you can choose your fate.

Fallen

Trial by fire. Forged by mist.
A declaration of love to a sweet tender kiss.
From the fallen, we have sought,
To bring Salvation from the start.
Let it be known, that tears will stop,
When the darkness envelops all that wrought.

I Am a Witness

I am a witness.

I watched the war of Heaven and Earth with my own eyes.

I saw everything. I felt everything.

What it meant to fear for your life. What it meant to watch everything you knew and loved burn to the ground. What it meant to lose your sense of identity.

I long for the days when everything appeared so much simpler.

> Before the battles.
>
> Before the hatred.
>
> Before the blood.
>
> Before the end of the world.
>
> That day…
>
> That day…

The day when crimson rained down upon the soil; When the bodies of those I held dear littered the ground; When the sky turned black and suffocating.

That day when I knew real anger and hatred for the first time.

That day when I shed my last tear.

The day I lost everything was the day I changed.

I never felt so useless. So small.

I may be a Fallen Angel, yet I am only human.

I can only be a witness.

www.ingramcontent.com/pod-product-compliance
Lightning Source LLC
La Vergne TN
LVHW010942200726
843509LV00013B/2264